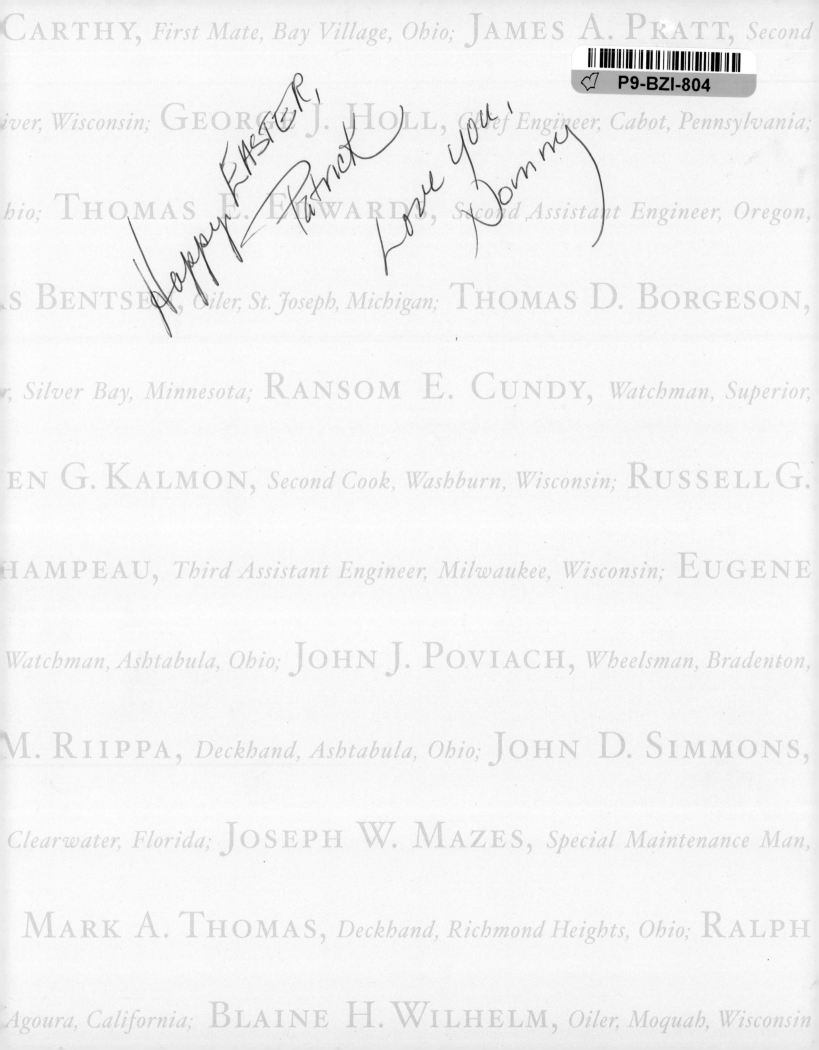

CARTHY, *First Mate, Bay Village, Ohio;* JAMES A. PRATT, *Second*

...ver, *Wisconsin;* GEORGE J. HOLL, *Chief Engineer, Cabot, Pennsylvania;*

...hio; THOMAS E. EDWARDS, *Second Assistant Engineer, Oregon,*

...s BENTSEN, *Oiler, St. Joseph, Michigan;* THOMAS D. BORGESON,

..., *Silver Bay, Minnesota;* RANSOM E. CUNDY, *Watchman, Superior,*

...EN G. KALMON, *Second Cook, Washburn, Wisconsin;* RUSSELL G.

...HAMPEAU, *Third Assistant Engineer, Milwaukee, Wisconsin;* EUGENE

Watchman, Ashtabula, Ohio; JOHN J. POVIACH, *Wheelsman, Bradenton,*

...M. RIIPPA, *Deckhand, Ashtabula, Ohio;* JOHN D. SIMMONS,

Clearwater, Florida; JOSEPH W. MAZES, *Special Maintenance Man,*

MARK A. THOMAS, *Deckhand, Richmond Heights, Ohio;* RALPH

Agoura, California; BLAINE H. WILHELM, *Oiler, Moquah, Wisconsin*

Happy Easter, Patrick! Love you, Tommy

THE EDMUND FITZGERALD

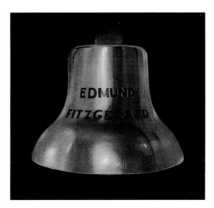

Song of the Bell

BY KATHY-JO WARGIN & ILLUSTRATED BY GIJSBERT VAN FRANKENHUYZEN

Author's Note

It is with sincere appreciation and gratitude that I thank Tom Farnquist, Executive Director of the Great Lakes Shipwreck Historical Society, for all of his guidance, input, and advice with this manuscript. This book could not have been done without your help. I would also like to thank all others who helped along the way, including the staff at the Petoskey Library, the staff at the Shipwreck Museum at Whitefish Point, my eight-year old son, Jake, for reading the manuscript and offering perspective through the eyes of a young reader, and to my husband, Ed Wargin, who helped every step of the way. Thank you.

Kathy-jo

Illustrator's Note

I want to thank the staff at both the Valley Camp Museum Ship in Sault St. Marie, Michigan, and the Willis B. Boyer Museum Ship in Toledo, Ohio, for letting me roam the ships. All of your helpful information became a valuable resource for the paintings in this book.

Many thanks go to Tom Farnquist and to the staff of the Shipwreck Coast Museum at Whitefish Point. The time and knowledge you shared with me was crucial to my research into and visual interpretation of this story.

Gijsbert

Text Copyright © 2003 Kathy-jo Wargin
Illustration Copyright © 2003 Gijsbert van Frankenhuyzen

Sleeping Bear Press™

315 E. Eisenhower Parkway, Ste. 200
Ann Arbor, MI 48108
www.sleepingbearpress.com

© 2003 Sleeping Bear Press is an imprint of Gale,
a part of Cengage Learning.

10 9 8 7 6 5 4 3

Library of Congress Cataloging-in-Publication Data
Wargin, Kathy-Jo.
The Edmund Fitzgerald : song of the bell / written by Kathy-Jo Wargin;
illustrated by Gijsbert van Frankenhuyzen.
p. cm.
Summary: Describes the voyage and sinking of the giant transport ship,
the Edmund Fitzgerald, which was caught in a raging storm while crossing
Lake Superior in November, 1975.
ISBN 978-1-58536-126-7
1. Edmund Fitzgerald (Ship)—Juvenile literature. 2. Shipwrecks-Superior,
Lake-Juvenile literature. [1. Edmund Fitzgerald (Ship) 2. Shipwrecks.]
I. Frankenhuyzen, Gijsbert van, ill. II. Title.
G530.E26 W37 2003
917.74'9043—dc22   2003013155
Printed by China Translation & Printing Services Limited, Guangdong Province, China. 3rd printing.   01/2010

Long, long ago, deep glaciers lay cold and hard upon the land. Over time, these huge walls of ice began to thaw and move away, scraping deep basins into the earth. As they pushed along, each large depression filled with water from the melting ice, giving birth to a large and powerful body of fresh water we now call the Great Lakes.

It was a warm Sunday afternoon on November 9, 1975. This was a time when people wore bell-bottom pants and platform shoes, and were learning a dance called the Hustle. Gerald R. Ford was president of the United States, a loaf of bread cost about 38 cents, and the waterways of the Great Lakes were filled with boats carrying coal, salt, lumber, and iron ore.

On this day, a group of sailors left port out of the Duluth-Superior Harbor in Superior, Wisconsin. That morning, the *Edmund Fitzgerald* had been loaded with 26 thousand tons of taconite pellets, which are tiny balls made from refined iron ore. This ore was to be taken to Zug Island in the Detroit River and used to build cars. This was the job of the men aboard the *Edmund Fitzgerald*, to safely transport taconite from the Iron Range of Minnesota to ports across the Great Lakes.

The bell rings forever where heroes are found,
for the soul of the sailor is held in its sound.

At 729 feet long, the *Edmund Fitzgerald* was the largest ship on the Great Lakes from the time it was launched in 1958 until larger ships came along in 1971. Through all its days, it was called the "Pride of the American Flag," and was the finest cargo ship on the Great Lakes. Because of this, only the best sailors in the fleet were offered the chance to work on board.

The ship plowed its way northeast in a slow, steady way. Captain Gerald "Ernest" McSorley knew that bad weather was blowing in because the weather bureau had issued a gale warning earlier that day. It was now early evening and he knew to pay close attention to the weather as they made their journey. Lake Superior is the deepest and largest of the Great Lakes, and its vast size could be troublesome when storms blow in.

But at the moment, this did not seem to bother Captain McSorley or his crew. They had experience with the wild storms of Lake Superior, and they knew their jobs well. So as the ship pushed on, the men kept busy with their duties. John Simmons, the wheelsman, steered the ship, while Nolan Church, the porter, helped serve meals in the ship's galley. John McCarthy, the first mate, assisted the captain while the cook polished the huge bell that sat on top of the pilothouse.

Every job on the ship was important, but it was usually a tradition for the cook to take care of the 200-pound bronze bell. The bell was buffed and shined to a beautiful golden luster, as if it were a brilliant crown.

The bell rang every four hours to announce a change
in the watch. Other times, it rang to warn of fog. And
when it did, it always rang with a rich and lovely sound,
reaching deep into the souls of the crewmen on board.

The soul of each sailor sang out in the chime
of the beautiful bell as it rang to keep time.

By nightfall, the *Edmund Fitzgerald* had traveled many miles. Captain McSorley knew that another ship carrying taconite, the *Arthur M. Anderson*, was traveling behind him. It had left port out of Two Harbors, Minnesota, and was heading to Gary, Indiana.

The two ships pushed on through midnight and into the early hours of morning.

As they did, the waves grew around them.

Black water whipped into a mass of confusion, striking out at the ship. The freshwater sea roared, and it was nearly impossible to tell the rain and snow from the tops of the waves.

But even as the storm raged around them, the 29 men aboard the *Edmund Fitzgerald* continued with their jobs, watchful and alert. And all the while, the bell remained steadfast as the wind blew all around it.

The men changed watch with the sound of the bell—
It rang through the storm as the freezing rain fell.

At nearly two in the morning, a voice came in over the *Edmund Fitzgerald*'s radio. It was Jesse "Bernie" Cooper, captain of the *Arthur M. Anderson*. He radioed Captain McSorley to talk about the bad weather. They were traveling close together, in the shelter of highlands on a northerly route along the Canadian shore rather than going straight across Lake Superior. Although this route was longer, it would be safer. So the pair pushed on, not knowing what would happen next.

The battered bell rang as the storm held its grip—
It rang for the men as the heart of the ship.

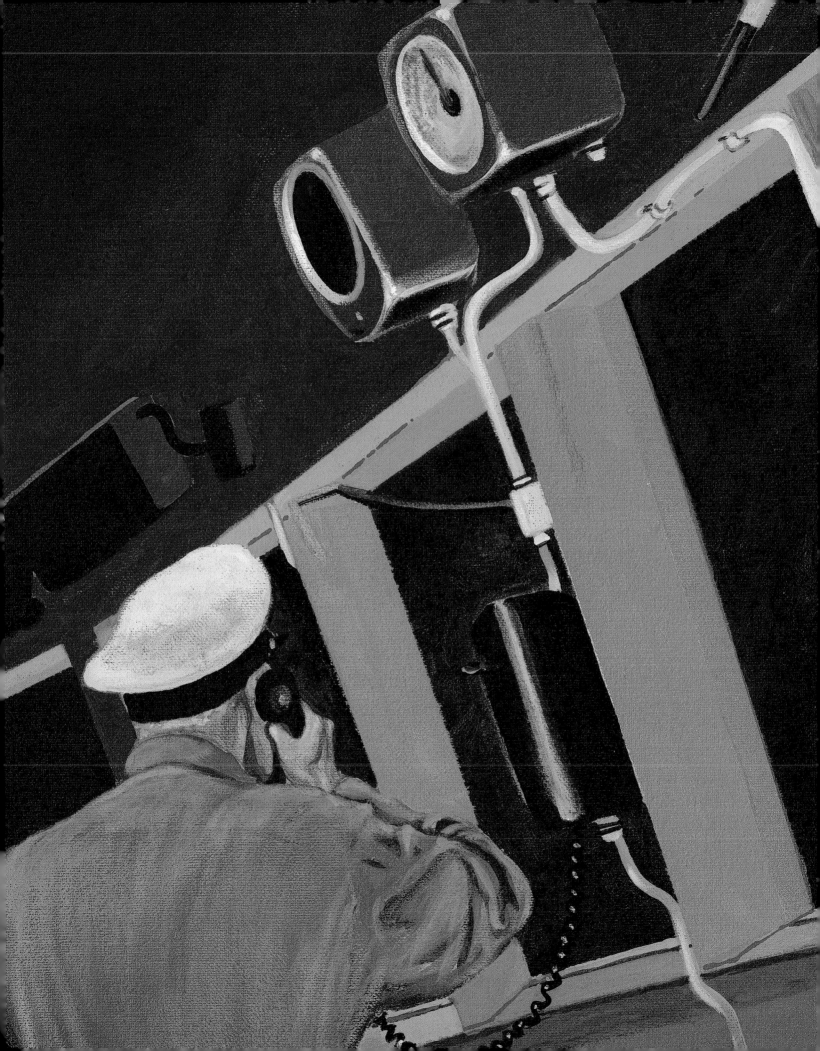

By early afternoon the next day, the *Edmund Fitzgerald* was far past Isle Royale and the Keweenaw Peninsula when something began to worry Captain McSorley. His long-range radar was not working, and he needed it to pass safely by Michipicoten Island and Caribou Island. These are dangerous areas to pass, and Captain McSorley knew he should not get in too close to Caribou Island because of Six Fathom Shoal, which is a hard, rocky shallow area that might tear the ship's hull into pieces.

The other ship, the *Arthur M. Anderson*, was about 16 miles behind the *Edmund Fitzgerald*. Captain Cooper of the *Anderson* watched his radar, noticing the path the *Fitzgerald* was taking as it rounded past Caribou Island.

Captain Cooper turned to his first mate Morgan Clark.

"Look at this, Morgan, the *Fitzgerald* is a lot closer to Six Fathom Shoal than I would like my ship to be."

**Minutes later, Captain McSorley of the *Fitzgerald*
radioed the *Anderson* and spoke to First Mate Clark.**

"*Anderson*, this is the *Fitzgerald*. I have sustained some topside damage. I have a fence rail laid down, two vents lost or damaged, and a starboard list. I'm checking down. Will you stay by me until I get to Whitefish?"

Captain Cooper replied, "Roger that, *Fitzgerald*.
Do you have your pumps going?"

"Yes," replied Captain McSorley, "*both of them.*"

As the ship moved on with a terrible list,
the bell still rang through the snow and the mist.

Captain Cooper was worried. A list meant the *Fitzgerald* was taking on water and leaning to one side. Damaged vents could mean water might pour into the ballast tanks, which are deep tanks on either side of the ship's cargo hold. These tanks can be filled with water when a ship is traveling light, to make the boat level and the journey safe. But the *Fitzgerald* was full of cargo. If it took on water, the weight could make the ship so heavy that it would sit dangerously low in the water.

"*Anderson*, this is the *Fitzgerald*. I have lost both radars. Can you provide me with radar plots till we reach Whitefish Bay?"

"Roger that, *Fitzgerald*," said the *Anderson*,
"we'll keep you advised of position."

The storm was heaving water upon the ship,
and now both long and short radar were gone!

Captain McSorley knew that the *Edmund Fitzgerald* had to make the sheltered lee of Whitefish Point. Getting there was his only hope, and the only hope for the other men as well. But as the *Edmund Fitzgerald* and the *Arthur M. Anderson* struggled east, the wind roared and the waves grew even larger.

With no radar, Captain McSorley used his radio direction finder to track a beacon signal from Whitefish Point, which assured him he was going in the right direction. The exhausted crew struggled to maintain the ship in the storm, trying to make it to Whitefish Bay. Captain McSorley was tracking his course when suddenly the radio direction beacon from Whitefish Point disappeared.

The storm had taken out the power to Whitefish Point! With no guiding radar or radio beacon, the *Fitzgerald* was blind in the storm.

It was dark and cold, and the *Edmund Fitzgerald* had to fight its way through the night.

No one was allowed on deck, and the men held onto the
hope that the *Fitzgerald* would make it to Whitefish Bay,
only 20 miles ahead.

At ten minutes past seven o'clock that night, First Mate Clark of the *Anderson* noticed a ship heading in the direction of the *Fitzgerald*. Because the *Anderson* was now acting as the eyes for the *Fitzgerald*, he radioed Captain McSorley to tell him that the ship would pass by safely.

After that, the first mate asked, "*Fitzgerald*, this is the *Anderson*, have you checked down?"

"Yes, we have," replied Captain McSorley.

"By the way, *Fitzgerald*, how are you making out with your problem?"

Captain McSorley replied, "We are holding our own."

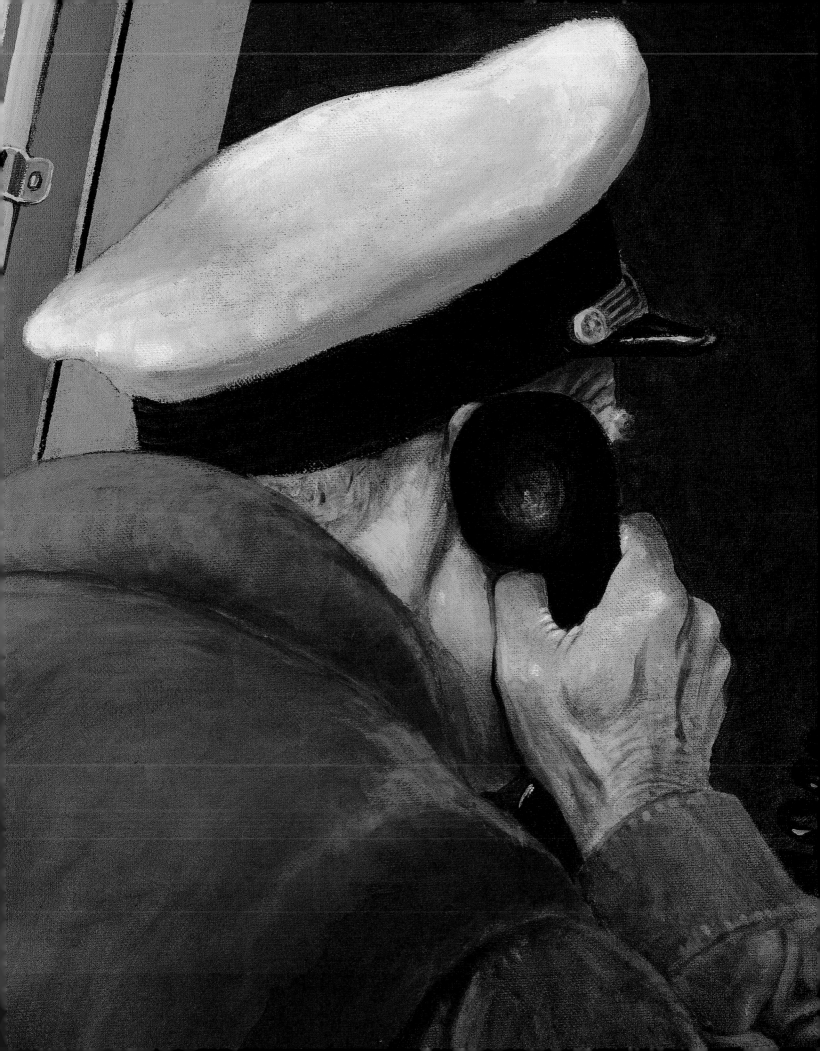

The first mate of the *Anderson* was watching the *Fitzgerald*'s progress on his radar when all of a sudden, the ship simply vanished from the screen. Captain Cooper ordered his men to search the horizon for the *Edmund Fitzgerald*.

But the men saw nothing.

The great ship could not be seen.

There in the blowing snow and pounding waves,
the *Edmund Fitzgerald* and the 29 men aboard
it disappeared without a cry for help.

There wasn't a sound except for the bell—
Some say it rang out when the mighty ship fell.

The *Edmund Fitzgerald* was found later, lying broken and twisted on the bottom of Lake Superior, only 17 miles from the shelter of Whitefish Point.

The great ship had plunged to the bottom so fast that no one may ever be sure what caused it to sink.

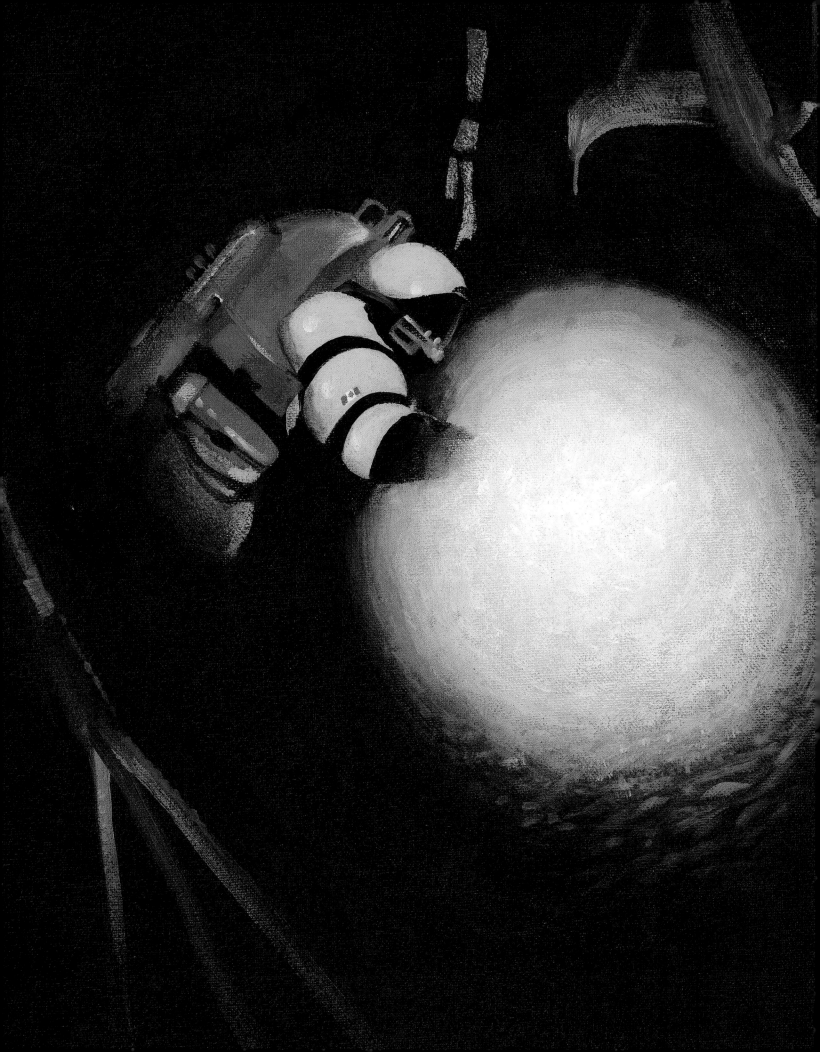

EPILOGUE

On July 4, 1995, twenty years after the tragic loss of the *Edmund Fitzgerald*, special divers went to the wreck to recover the bell from the ship. When the divers cut the bell free, it was hoisted to the surface. Along the way, as it swung on a cable, the bell chimed again for the sailors, ringing out beautifully as it broke the surface and came into the sunlight for the first time in so many years. A replica bell, inscribed with the names of the 29 men who died that night, was brought down to the ship where it will remain forever, as a tribute to those lost. Then, as a wreath of flowers was tossed upon the water, the family members said goodbye to the men they loved so much.

Today, the bell that rang out from the *Edmund Fitzgerald* that fateful night is lovingly polished once again, reminding us to honor those sailors and the heritage of our people. It is a heritage of water, of wind, of ships, and of hardworking men and women. And once a year, on the anniversary of the wreck, the bell rings out 30 times, one time for each of the 29 men lost that night, and one last time for all mariners lost on the Great Lakes.

The bell rings forever where heroes are found,
for the soul of the sailor is held in its sound.

We tell them good-bye with a loving farewell,
but their legend lives on...in the song of the bell.

The Bell as a Memorial

The families of the *Edmund Fitzgerald*'s crew were very sad when the ship was lost. The crewmen died suddenly and unexpectedly, never to be recovered. There wasn't a way to have a proper funeral for them.

In November of 1994, the family members asked the Great Lakes Shipwreck Historical Society to help them create a memorial to the lost crew of the *Fitzgerald*. The families met Tom Farnquist, Executive Director of the Shipwreck Society, at the Mariners' Church in Detroit, Michigan.

At the meeting, everyone thought that one important artifact from the shipwreck should be brought to the surface—the ship's bell.

The *Fitzgerald* lies in Canadian waters. Permission to raise the bell had to be secured from the Canadian government. A letter, encouraging that permission be given, was sent from the office of the president of the United States. The family members also wrote letters in support of the effort to raise the bell.

With the help of Emory Kristof of the National Geographic Society, the Canadian Navy provided a ship and crew of 85 to the bell recovery expedition, with two mini-submarines aboard. The expedition also used the NEWTSUIT, a high-tech underwater diving suit. The NEWTSUIT allowed a diver to get close enough to the bell to carefully remove it from the roof of the pilothouse.

The bell of the *Edmund Fitzgerald* was recovered from the ship, lying in 535 feet of water, on July 4, 1995. A replica bell, engraved with the names of the lost crewmembers, was put back in its place. The replica bell is still on the ship today, serving as a grave marker for the crew.

The *Edmund Fitzgerald*'s bell is at the Great Lakes Shipwreck Museum at Whitefish Point, Michigan, just 17 miles from where the ship lies in Lake Superior. Many people come to visit this museum and see the bell. "Now," said the families, "we have a place to come where we can remember our loved ones."

—Great Lakes Shipwreck Historical Society

ERNEST M. MCSORLEY, *Master, Toledo, Ohio;* JOHN H. M

Mate, Lakewood, Ohio; MICHAEL E. ARMAGOST, *Third Mate, Iron*

EDWARD F. BINDON, *First Assistant Engineer, Fairport Harbor,*

Ohio; FREDERICK J. BEETCHER, *Porter, Superior, Wisconsin;* THOM

AB Maintenance Man, Duluth, Minnesota; NOLAN F. CHURCH, *Por*

Wisconsin; BRUCE L. HUDSON, *Deckhand, North Olmsted, Ohio;* AL

HASKELL, *Second Assistant Engineer, Millbury, Ohio;* OLIVER J. C

W. O'BRIEN, *Wheelsman, St. Paul, Minnesota;* KARL A. PECKOL

Florida; ROBERT C. RAFFERTY, *Steward, Toledo, Ohio;* PAUL

Wheelsman, Ashland, Wisconsin; GORDON F. MACLELLAN, *Wip*

Ashland, Wisconsin; WILLIAM J. SPENGLER, *Watchman, Toledo, Oh*

G. WALTON, *Oiler, Fremont, Ohio;* DAVID E. WEISS, *Cadet (Deck*